Be Brave

Biblical stories of faith & courage

BY MARJIE SCHAEFER

www.flourishthroughtheword.com

© 2016 by Marjie Schaefer. All rights reserved. No part of this document may be reproduced or transmitted in any form by any means, electronic, mechanical, photocopying, recording, or otherwise, without prior written permission of Marjie Schaefer.

Dedication

The summer of 2016 held many surprises for me and my family. We were blessed to visit the land of Israel for the first time, and while there, experienced the amazing truth of the Gospels as we stood in the same places Jesus had stood. What a privilege and blessing to see His homeland with our own eyes and to see the same things He saw while on earth.

After we returned home, I was hit with a severe illness that included a hospitalization and over five weeks in bed. It was during this time that my family rallied to my aid. They offered on-going help, support, love and encouragement. They showed me what it's like to be brave.

Along with my family's support, I was on the receiving end of a mighty out-pouring of love, support and ministry from the greater Body of Christ. It was God's grace to me at a very needy time in my life. At my lowest moments physically, it was the prayers of my brothers and sisters in Christ that carried me. These friends also showed me what it's like to be brave.

Sometimes bravery comes in many different forms. I am grateful for the bravery I witnessed this summer.

I express my deepest gratitude and affection to:

Steve, Hayley, Jordan, Matthew and Luke Schaefer

The Flourish leadership team and community

Evergreen Community Church

This Bible study was written through your on-going encouragement and on the wings of your prayers!

It is dedicated to you!

With love from,
Marjie

What is bravery?

The famous actor, John Wayne, is quoted as saying, "Courage is being scared to death, but saddling up anyway!"

Have you ever felt that way?

Have you ever faced something inevitable that required a huge amount of courage on your part, and the only solution for you was to step out in faith and just do it?

Google is replete with amazing quotations on bravery. I know that all of us could go on-line and find great and Pinterest-worthy sayings that would be very inspirational in our own quest for bravery. But when push comes to shove, all the pithy quotes in the world won't actually do the deed for you. There comes a time when each of us just has to 'saddle up anyway'.

What can we do to cultivate bravery and courage in our own lives?

Certainly there are countless examples of brave people that could spur us on. The Bible itself is filled with them! This study will have us examine some of them: Paul, Timothy, Moses, Daniel, Abraham and Sarah, and Jesus Himself. I have also included some modern-day examples of bravery for our encouragement.

I honestly believe that the surest way to bravery is to live a life based on the promises of the Word of God. Not only has He given us countless examples in His Word of men and women who were called upon to do seemingly impossible things (Hello! Daniel in the lion's den!), but He has shown us that as we step out, He gives us grace upon grace for each second of challenge we may face, and He goes with us in the midst of it all.

But how will we know all of this if we do not open up His Word and discover His amazing provisions for ourselves?

The truth is, the Lord Himself has even called us to be brave: "...wait patiently for the Lord, be brave and courageous." (Psalm 27:14)

I encourage you to take these next 5 weeks and determine to dig into the Word and glean all that you can from His precious promises. Start each week in worship with the hymns provided. Let's all be brave together,

Marjie

Be Brave
WEEK ONE

*Obedience is
the great opener of eyes*

The blind man is healed by Jesus

Amazing Grace

*Amazing grace! How sweet the sound—
that saved a wretch like me!
I once was lost but now am found,
was blind but now I see.*

*'Twas grace that taught my heart to fear,
and grace my fears relieved;
How precious did that grace appear,
the hour I first believed.*

*The Lord has promised good to me,
His word my hope secures;
He will my shield and portion be,
as long as life endures.*

*Thru many dangers, toils, and snares,
I have already come;
'Tis grace hat brought me safe thus far,
and grace will lead me home.*

*When we've been there ten thousand years,
bright shining as the sun,
We've no less days to sing God's praise,
than when we'd first begun.*

John Newton; John P. Rees, stanza 5
Traditional American melody

Day One:

Read all of John chapter 9 today to get the full story of Jesus' interaction with the blind man. After you do, answer the following questions:

1) <u>Where</u> is Jesus as this story takes place?
2) <u>Who</u> is with Him?
3) <u>What</u> one or two things stand out to you in this text as you read it?

Get ready! We have much more to 'see' as we dig in for days 2-5!

Day Two:

Read John 9:1-7 and answer the following:

1) How did Jesus answer His disciple's questions regarding the potential sin of the blind man and his parents? (Hint: 3 specific things)

2) Why do you think the disciples assumed his blindness was due to sin? Use Scripture to support your answer.

Greek Word: Works, ergon (er-gon) Strong's #2041: Compare the words energy and urge. Toil, occupation, enterprise, deed, task, accomplishment, work, labor, course of action.

The miraculous works of Jesus are the works of God that imply power and might.

3) What was the 'work' Jesus was sent to do? See John 4:34; John 5:19 and 36 to help you answer.

4) What did Jesus specifically do in John 9:6? Why do you think He did this?

5) What did Jesus tell the blind man to do?

6) What does 'Siloam' mean? Why do you think this is significant?

> *"Cheer up now, you faint-hearted warrior! Not only has Christ traveled the road, but He has defeated your enemies."*
>
> ~Charles Spurgeon

Day Three:

Read John 9:8-12 to answer today's questions.

1) Why do you think the healing of the blind man was such a big deal for all of his neighbors?

2) What is the blind man's 3-step testimony as stated in verse 11?

3) What makes this former blind man so brave?

4) What can you learn and emulate from his bravery?

Day Four:

Read John 9:13-34 for today.

1) After reading this entire section, what title would you give to this passage and why?

2) What is the significance of the day Jesus performed the miracle and why are the Pharisees so upset by it? Use Scripture to support your answer.

3) Verse 18 reveals a critical stumbling block for the Jews, what is it?

4) Describe the behavior of the blind man's parents. Why did they say and do these things?

5) In verses 30-33, the former blind man again shares his testimony and the joy of his heart with the accusing and demanding Pharisees. He makes a powerful statement in verse 31: "Now we know that God does not hear sinners." Does his statement bother you? Why or why not?

6) The Jews, prior to the New Testament being written, drew their belief system from the Old Testament. When Jesus came and lived among them, He declared that He had come to fulfill the Law.

Here are two examples of what the Old Testament has to say about sinners and God:

"The Lord is far from the wicked and distances Himself from them, but He hears the prayer of the consistently righteous, that is those with spiritual integrity and moral courage." (Proverbs 15:29 Amplified Bible)

"Then they will cry to the Lord, but He will not answer them; instead, He will even hide His face from them at that time, withholding His mercy, because they have practiced and tolerated and ignored evil acts." (Micah 3:4 Amplified Bible)

It is very important for us to pause here and reflect on the words of the blind man in verse 31 and to glean a greater context of the belief system of the people of Jesus' day.

The blind man went on to say, "...but if anyone is a worshiper of God and does His will, He hears him." (John 9:31)

- From your own personal experience with Jesus, how would you explain verse 31 to someone who is searching to be right with God?

- What are some other examples in the Bible of people who got right with God through the truth revealed in Jesus Christ?

- What was so unique about this miracle and what the people in this story experienced according to verse 31?

- What was the conclusion of the blind man?

- What ultimately happened to the 'blind' man at the hands of the religious leaders?

- Who were the ones who were really 'blind'?

> **"Amazing grace, how sweet the sound!**
> **I once was lost but now am found,**
> **Was blind but now I see!"**

Day Five:

Read John 9:35-41 today.

1) Why do you think Jesus went to find the formerly blind man when He learned he had been cast out from the temple? (Use John 1:7 and John 16:31 to help you answer)

2) In verse 38, the man has a new testimony. What is it and what is the 'fruit' of his testimony?

3) Explain what Jesus meant in verse 39, and use the following Scriptures to help you answer as well as any other verses that come to mind:

- John 3:17:
- John 5:22 & 27:
- Matthew 13:13
- Matthew 15:14

4) Some of the Pharisees who were with Jesus at the time seemed troubled by His words. Perhaps their hearts were convicted by the words of the "Living Word". From everything you've studied in this chapter, what can you conclude Jesus was saying to the Pharisees about their spiritual state?

5) Why do you think the healed blind man was brave?

A Modern Story of Bravery
Jim and Elisabeth Elliot

Jim Elliot became a believer in Jesus at the age of six. He was raised by parents who were devoted to the Gospel and encouraged him to be adventurous as he lived for Christ. As a young adult, he felt called to share Jesus with the Quechua Indians of Ecuador. While working with them, he heard of an unreached, violent group of indigenous people, the Aucas, whose name means 'savage'.

After several tries in reaching this group, and in spite of their seeming friendliness, Jim Elliot and four additional missionaries were speared to death when they finally made contact with the Aucas.

Jim Elliot's short life and the lives of the other men who were killed, became a powerful witness around the world as they were featured in newspapers and magazines.

Jim's wife, Elisabeth, became a noted author and speaker as she wrote his life story in the two biographies that describe his life and death, Shadow of the Almighty and Through Gates of Splendor. These stories became a clarion call for a new generation to take the Gospel all over the world.

Elisabeth and her baby daughter opted to stay in the jungles of Ecuador, and she eventually led the very tribe that had murdered her husband to the Lord!

Jim Elliot's bravery can be summed up by the motto he sought to live by: "He is no fool who gives what he cannot keep to gain that which he cannot lose."

Jim and Elisabeth's love for Jesus and the gospel enabled them to be brave.

Be Brave
WEEK TWO

The practical theology of being brave

O God, Our Help in Ages Past

O God, our help in ages past, our hope for years to come,
Our shelter from the stormy blast, and our eternal home.

Under the shadow of Thy throne, Thy saints have dwelt secure;
Sufficient is Thine arm alone, and our defense is sure.

Before the hills in order stood, or earth received her frame,
From everlasting Thou art God, to endless years the same.

A thousand ages in Thy sight are like an evening gone;
Short as the watch that ends the night before the rising sun.

Time, like an ever rolling stream, bears all its sons away;
They fly, forgotten, as a dream dies at the op'ning day.

O God, our help in ages past, our hope for years to come,
Be Thou our guard while life shall last, and our eternal home.

~Isaac Watts and William Croft

Day One:

It's one thing to live a life of bravery and courage, but what does God's Word have to say about it?

This week, we will be examining Scriptures that give us an underlying foundation of truth for walking out our days in bravery and faith on the earth.

1) Before we begin, write out your personal definition of bravery:

2) Read Psalm 91 and answer the following questions:
   - Where do we find true safety?

   - What is something practical we can say to the Lord each day?

   - In verses 3 & 4, what are the promises made to us?

3) Read Psalm 112:7 and Isaiah 43:2 along with Psalm 91:5. Write out the specifics from all three verses. Read them in different translations (YouVersion Bible App—or—biblegateway.com) and choose your favorite wording:

4) In Psalm 91:6-7, what are the other specific things we are not to fear?

Day Two:

Read all of Psalm 91 again.

1) In verses 9-16, there are 3 'because' statements. What are they? Write them out along with the verse references:

2) How do you specifically make the Lord 'your dwelling place'? What does that mean to you? Be prepared to share with your group.

3) How do you set your love upon the Lord? What does this mean for us practically as we seek to walk with Him each day?

4) What does it mean to 'know' the Lord's name?

5) Does this psalm promise us total immunity from calamity? Why or why not?

"If you are really humble, if you realize how small you are and how much you need God, then you cannot fail." ~Mother Teresa

Day Three:

Read Psalm 91 again.

1) Take the time today to write out your personal prayer based on this amazing psalm—or—write out a Biblical declaration based on this psalm that you can say over your life and the life of your loved ones.

2) Hebrews chapter 11 lists some of the great heroes of faith in the Old Testament. In verses 4-35, we read about amazing blessings and tremendous victories achieved through faith. In verses 36-38, we read about those who through faith endured great trial, suffering and persecution.

The walk of faith is the glorious process of becoming free in Jesus! By faith in the resurrection of Jesus, we become free from the fear of death. Through faith in Jesus being our 'high priest', we know that we have a Savior who can understand and sympathize with us. By faith in Jesus' work of holiness in our lives, we can be free to enter into God's Presence boldly and without hesitation.

Read the entire chapter of Hebrews 11 today. Write out a Biblical definition of faith based on verses 1-3:

Greek Word: Framed, katartizo (Kat-ar-tid-zoe); Strong's #2675: to arrange, set up in order, equip, adjust, complete what is lacking, make fully ready, repair, prepare.

3) Using the Greek definition for the word 'framed', write out what it means to have your world framed by the Word of God.

Day Four:

Read Hebrews 11: 4-22 and answer the questions for today:

1) What did Abel's offering to God signify?

2) What was significant about Enoch?

3) Verse 6 is a hallmark verse for Jesus-followers. Look it up in several translations and write in your own words what this verse means to you. How are you living it out?

4) How do Noah's actions reveal his faith?

5) Share specifically how their faith played a transforming role in the lives of Abraham and Sarah.

6) How would you explain verses 13-16 to someone who might be struggling with their faith?

7) How did the following patriarchs express their faith as seen in verses 17-22:
    - Abraham:
    - Isaac:
    - Jacob:
    - Joseph:

8) In this brief biological look at these Bible heroes, what is the common denominator that led to their brave action?

Day Five:

Read Hebrews 11:23-40 and answer the following questions:

1) How does the story of Moses' faith begin?

2) What 6 choices did Moses make listed in verses 23-29 because of his faith? List them here. Do you think those choices required bravery?

3) There is a key listed in this passage that enabled Moses to endure. What is it? Can you connect it to verse 1 of this passage?

4) Of the names mentioned in verses 30-32, which individual stands out to you? Take the time to cross-reference their story and read it in the Old Testament.

5) What 10 things were accomplished through the faith of those listed in verses 33-35?

6) Does faith automatically guarantee us an exemption from hardships? Provide a Biblical proof-text for your answer based on your study of this passage.

7) How does Biblical faith enable us to be brave?

Faith is not a bridge over troubled waters, but it is a pathway through them.

A Modern Story of Bravery
Mother Teresa

Mother Teresa heard the distinct and life-altering call of God on her life in. His message to her was clear: Go and live and work among the poorest of the poor.

Her mother was initially against the idea of her leaving home to become a nun. Later, she grew to understand her daughter's calling and as she told her goodbye, these were her words, "Put your hand in His hand and walk all alone with Him."

The Lord led her to live and minister in India. For seventeen years she lived in Calcutta and taught at St. Mary's High School. She loved teaching and she claimed she was the happiest nun in the world.

Later she left that post and it became the greatest sacrifice and the hardest thing she had ever done. Yet she vowed to follow what she believed was God's will for her, and she left for the slums of Calcutta.

She would open a home for the dying and an orphanage. At the heart of her ministry was her deeply held belief that everything she did, she did for the love of God. It was not the broken, dying bodies of the poor that she tended to, but rather, to Jesus Himself, coming to her in the disguise of the poor.

She chose a life of poverty for herself and she would always strive toward greater humility, in an effort to fulfill her vow to joyfully give 'wholehearted and free service to the poorest of the poor.'

She won numerous awards for her work, including the Nobel Peace Prize in 1979, which she accepted in the name of the poor and unloved everywhere. What Mother Teresa began with a handful of ministers has grown to an order that is active in more than 130 countries, running a worldwide network of shelters for the poor and homeless, orphanages, AIDS hospices, clinics for lepers, homes for unwed mothers, and other places of charity.

Her love for Jesus enabled her to be brave.

Be Brave
WEEK THREE

A Blueprint for Bravery
Paul and Timothy

How Firm a Foundation

How firm a foundation, ye saints of the Lord,
Is laid for your faith in His excellent Word!
What more can He say than to you He hath said,
To you who for refuge to Jesus have fled?

Fear not, I am with thee; O be not dismayed,
For I am thy God, and will still give thee aid;
I'll strengthen thee, help thee, and cause thee to stand,
Upheld by My righteous, omnipotent hand.

When through fiery trials thy pathway shall lie,
My grace, all sufficient, shall be thy supply.
The flame shall not hurt thee; I only design
Thy dross to consume and thy gold to refine.

The soul that on Jesus hath leaned for repose
I will not, I will not desert to its foes;
That soul, though all hell should endeavor to shake,
I'll never, no, never, no, never forsake!

~Rippons Selection of Hymns, Traditional American Melody

Day One:

Read 2 Timothy 1: 1-14 and answer the following questions:

1) What did Paul say about himself and what 3 things gave him his assurance?

2) What did Paul say about Timothy and to Timothy in following verses:
   - Verse 2-
   - Verse 3-
   - Verse 4-
   - Verse 5-
   - Verse 6-

3) Write out 2 Timothy 1:7:

Greek Word: sound mind, sophronisos (so-fron-is-moss); Strong's #4995: Safe-thinking; the word denotes good judgment, disciplined thought patterns and the ability to understand and make right decisions. It includes the qualities of self-control and self-discipline.

- What 3 things has God given to us according to this verse?

- If someone struggles with a spirit of fear, what is a natural conclusion we can make as to where the fear comes from?

4) Look up the following verses and list out further insights into battling a spirit of fear:
   - Romans 8:15-16:
   - 1 John 4:18:
   - Acts 1:8:
   - 1 John 5:4:

5) What points does Paul make to Timothy in verse 8? Have you ever felt ashamed of the Gospel?

6) What are we to remember about our God according to verses 9-10?

7) List out the specific things you learn from Paul's encouragement to Timothy in verses 11-14:

8) What was the basis of Paul's courage?

"Success is not final; failure is not fatal: it is the courage to continue that counts."

~Winston Churchill

Day Two:

Read 2 Timothy 2: 1-13.

1) Devotion to God, as well as bravery, grows as we learn to depend upon the Holy Spirit's life in us through His indwelling Presence. Where is our strength rooted according to verse 1? What does this mean to you, and what are some practical ways that you are strong in Jesus?

2) 2 Timothy 2:2 gives us a specific pattern for passing along our faith to others. List out the 4 generations Paul mentions in this verse:
   1-
   2-
   3-
   4-

   Have you been invested in or discipled? Where do you fit in the 4-generation cycle? Are you a 'Paul' to someone who is younger in the faith? Who is your 'Paul'?

   Be prepared to tell about your Paul/Timothy relationship in your group.

3) How does a disciple-making relationship give us courage for life?

4) In verses 3-6, Paul tells that as ministers (this applies to each one of us!), we must endure hardship. What are the 3 metaphors he gives, and what are the duties attached to each:

5) In verses 8-13, Paul expands the concept of suffering, as he gives the experience of Jesus as the example to all of us. What did Christ go through according to verse 8? What is the desired outcome of Paul's suffering for the sake of the Gospel?

6) Paul reinforces the principle of present suffering in verses 11-13. What elements in these verses are a call for courage, bravery, and endurance?

Day Three:

Read 2 Timothy 2: 14-22.

1) Human beings need to be reminded of the truth. Why is this, according to verse 14?

2) Write out the specific actions of verse 15:

3) In verse 15, Paul uses the metaphor of an unashamed worker. What does it mean for the worker to rightly divide the Word of truth?

4) How have you prepared yourself to be an unashamed worker?

5) Look up the following Scriptures and summarize what each verse says in the space provided. Use your notes to craft a paragraph that communicates the importance of knowing and handling the Word of truth properly:
   - John 6:63:
   - Hebrews 4:12:
   - 1 Corinthians 2:13, 14:
   - John 8:31-32:
   - Psalm 19:10:
   - 1 Timothy 4:13:
   - Psalm 119:11:
   - Ephesians 6:17:
   - 2 Timothy 3:16-17:

6) Why do you think rightly dividing the Word of truth is so important in our quest to be brave?

Day Four:

Read 2 Timothy 2:16-26.

1) What is the fruit of profane and idle babblings as seen in verses 16-18?

2) In verses 19-22, Paul describes a great house (which is a metaphor for the professing church) shoe foundation is safe because God has put His seal on it. List out the spiritual applications you see from these verses, and relate them to your personal life.

3) What are we to avoid in verse 23?

4) How does this reflect the other verses we have studies so far in this chapter?
    - Verse 7:
    - Verse 14:
    - Verse 15:
    - Verse 16:

5) How should a servant of the Lord be characterized according to verses 24-25?

6) What can happen to those who oppose the truth of Gods Word and follow false teachers?

Day Five:

The Source of our bravery—Jesus!

Through our identification with Christ in his death, burial, and resurrection, we have won the victory!

1) Jesus is the center of the Gospel message. List out what is He identified as in the 3 passages of Scripture:
    - Romans 1:3-6:
    - Matthew 1: 18-25:
    - Hebrews 2:10:

2) What are the 5 stages in our salvation experience based on 2 Thessalonians 2: 13-14?

3) Once we enter into a saving relationship with Jesus, what becomes the outcome of our faith in Him as seen in Romans 6:15-18?

4) What an incredible heritage and future we have in and through Jesus! We know it was not an easy road for Him, as we have seen He was both fully man and fully God from our study above. At the darkest moment in His life, bravery and courage was required of Him.

Read the 2 Scripture passages that reveal some of the final hours of Jesus' life on the earth and write down your thoughts and reflections from these passages: Luke 22: 39-46 and John 19: 28-30:

From all of the study we have done, we culminate today with the birth, life, and death of Jesus. He is the ultimate brave one! He died for the sins of you and me, and then He was raised from the dead. This miracle event of a substitutionary death and victorious resurrection constitutes the Gospel.

This is the Gospel we preach!

The truth of the Gospel makes us brave!

"I am not ashamed of the Gospel of Christ, for it is the power of God to salvation for everyone who believes…" (Romans 1:16)

No storm can shake my inmost calm, while to the Rock I'm clinging. Since Christ is Lord of heaven and earth, How can I keep from singing?
~Robert Lowry

A Modern Story of Bravery
Azzam

Azzam is a former pirate somewhere in Somalia today, who rides in coffins under corpses, because he knows Somali Muslims will not open a casket or touch a dead body, much less look under it. So Azzam 'safely' rides in caskets underneath corpses traveling outside of Somalia where he then is given a load of Bibles in Kenya. He travels back into Somalia in a coffin, under a corpse, with the precious cargo of god's Word that many people in his area are desperate to read. How could he have ever come to the decision to engage in such a dangerous mission?

Azzam was born and raised a Muslim but was having dreams of Jesus. He had sought out his imam for answers, but the man violently berated and beat him. When his mother found out he as having Jesus dreams, she commanded him to leave the home for his own protection and never come back. That's exactly what he did. He walked miles and miles, quite sure his father would be unable to find him.

But he was wrong. His father was a powerful warlord who located him quickly and sent Azzam a package. When he opened the package he was sickened to learn that his mother had been killed. A photograph was included inside which showed his mother kneeling in front of two men who had their knives raised over her. The day Azzam opened the package is the day he embraced Jesus Christ as his Lord and Savior.

Azzam went so far as to seek out the two men who murdered his mother. He told them that he forgave them. He told them that Jesus loved them and that He could forgive murderers. Through his reaching out, the two men gave their lives to Christ. Then they confided to Azzam, "As we killed your mother, her last words were, 'Jesus, Jesus, I love You.'

Heaven has been and is being moved by these radical followers of Jesus. The forgiveness and love of Jesus Christ has empowered Azzam to be brave.

Be Brave
WEEK FOUR

Bravery from the knees up
The Story of Daniel

'Tis So Sweet To Trust in Jesus

*'Tis so sweet to trust in Jesus,
just to take Him at His word,
Just to rest upon His promise,
Just to know 'thus saith the Lord.'*

*Refrain:
Jesus, Jesus, how I trust Him!
How I've proved Him o'er and o'er!
Jesus, Jesus, precious Jesus!
O for grace to trust Him more!*

*O how sweet to trust in Jesus,
just to trust His cleansing blood,
Just in simple faith to plunge me
'neath the healing, cleansing flood!*

Refrain

*Yes, 'tis sweet to trust in Jesus,
just from sin and self to cease,
Just from Jesus simply taking life
and rest and joy and peace.*

Refrain

*I'm so glad I learned to trust Him,
precious Jesus, Savior Friend;
And I know that He is with me,
will be with me to the end.*

Refrain

~Louisa M. R. Stead and William J. Kirkpatrick

Day One:

Daniel is a brave example of a man who demonstrated real faith through his decades of life-and-death choices.

He spent his early years growing up in Jerusalem. His name means "God is my judge." Even as a teenager in the opening chapter of the book of Daniel, his appears strong and well-developed. As will see in this week's study, his faith was called upon again and again to make brave choices.

His prayer life was the hallmark of his brave life.

Read Daniel 1 and answer the following questions:

1) What happened to the city of Jerusalem?

2) Describe Daniel and his friends.

3) Why were they put into a 3-year training program?

4) What did Daniel do in verse 8? Why do you think he would make a stand like this?

5) What do you learn from verse 9? What application can you personally glean from this verse?

6) Summarize what happens to Daniel and his friends in verses 10-16.

7) What was their source of knowledge and skill?

8) What did the king discover after examining Daniel and his friends?

9) How does our theme of be brave figure into this story?

Day Two:

Daniel's brave choice to not eat the kings' food was blessed by God and this ultimately set Daniel apart.

"God gave them knowledge….and Daniel had understanding in all visions and dreams." (Daniel 1:17)

Read Daniel 2: 1-49.

1) Bullet point and list out the events of verses 1-13.

2) Do you think the king actually remembered his dream, or was this a test to see if his wise men had supernatural ability?

3) What did Daniel do immediately upon getting a delay on the decree from the king?

4) How did the Lord provide for Daniel?

5) Read Daniels' response in verses 20-23. Write out the sentence or phrase that you can use today as your praise to God.

6) As Daniel went to the king, <u>who</u> did he say was ultimately responsible for the answer the king needed? <u>Why</u> was the secret revealed?

7) In what 2 ways did the king respond?

8) How was God glorified by Daniel's faith and bravery?

Day Three:

The years in Babylon continued for Daniel and now there's a new king in power, Darius.

Read Daniel 6.

1) What 2 things do you learn about Daniel in verses 1-4?

2) What did the government officials (satraps) perceive about Daniel?

   What did they perceive about Darius?

   What did they scheme as a result?

3) What do you learn about Daniel in verse 10? How is this an act of bravery for Daniel?

4) What happened as a result of Daniel's bravery?

5) How did Darius respond to his own decree? What possible conclusions can you draw from his actions (see verses 18-20)?

6) What did God do for Daniel?

7) What 3 responses did King Darius have as a result?

Day Four:

Daniel chose to trust God repeatedly, regardless of how difficult or dangerous the situation appeared to be. Daniel knew that God is God. Daniel knew that when he prayed, a Living Person, a personally-engaged God, was listening and would respond to him. Daniel had a personal and dynamic relationship with God.

Today we will peer into his personal devotional life and take a look at his prayer for the people.

Read Daniel 9: 1-19.
   1) How is it that Daniel 'understood' the word of the Lord?

2) What did he do in response to this understanding?

3) What are the first 2 things you see in Daniel's prayer that we can also utilize in our prayer lives?

4) In verses 5-11, what specific sins does Daniel confess? List them here.

5) Why do you think it was important for Daniel to confess the sins of his people and his nation? Do you think this applies to us?

6) What did the Lord do in response to the sins of Israel?

7) After his specific confession, Daniel then makes intercession—or specific requests of the Lord. List them here.

8) Read and write out 2 Chronicles 7:14:

"You gain strength, courage and confidence by every experience in which you really stop to look fear in the face. You must do the thing you think you cannot do"
~Eleanor Roosevelt

Day Five:

We have seen from examining Daniel's prayer in chapter 9 that he confessed sin on behalf of his nation and his people. Did you notice the pronouns that he used?

Daniel was aware of the sin in his own heart, but he also prayed on behalf of the hearts of the people.

As the people of God, we long to see revival sweep our nation and also our world. Perhaps it is time to stop pointing our finger at others and deal with the sin in our own hearts so the Lord can pour out His Spirit in even greater degrees.

Many years ago, there was a revivalist preacher named Gypsy Smith. He was asked where revival begins. He answered: "I draw a circle around myself and make sure everything in that circle is right with God."

Today we will 'draw a circle' around ourselves and ask the Lord to prepare our hearts for whatever He wants to do. Revival is deeply personal and it starts at the individual level.

Today we will prepare our hearts for revival.

Hosea 10:12 says: "Break up your unplowed ground; for it is time to seek the Lord, until He comes and showers righteousness on you."

The list provided on the next few pages was authored by another old-time preacher of decades ago. He asked his readers to look to our own hearts and the spiritual ground that perhaps needs to be 'plowed up' by the Lord.

Let me tell you friends, it will take a step of bravery to take the time to carefully go through this list before the Lord!

This list is not comfortable. This list is convicting.

But as we take the time to prayerfully sit before the Lord and ask His Holy Spirit to speak to us and convict us in any areas that need to be surrendered to Him, we will see that promised 'shower of righteousness' He speaks of in Hosea 10:12.

So spend some time in prayer, asking the Lord to prepare your heart. Get quiet before Him, and allow His Spirit to speak to your heart. It is time to seek the Lord!

Please read the message at the end of the list once you finish.

List:

Ingratitude: List all the blessings and favors God has given to you, before and after salvation. Which ones have I forgotten to thank Him for?

Losing Love for God: Consider how devastated I would be if my husband, children or other loved ones not only were lessened in their love for me, but increasingly loved someone or something else more. Is there any evidence I am lessening in my love for God?

Neglect of Bible reading: Has my Bible reading been pushed aside by an over-full schedule? As I read my Bible, am I consistently preoccupied with other things? How long has it been since reading my Bible was a delight? Do I read it so casually that I don't even remember what it said when I finish?

Neglect of Prayer: Have I substituted wishing, daydreaming, or fantasizing for real prayer? Is my faith focused on Him as I pray?

Lack of concern for the souls of others: Have I become so politically correct that I don't apply the Gospel to those I know and love? Or am I so consumed in my own life and problems, that I fail to see others around me who are desperate for Jesus, yet I am not praying for them or warning them?

Neglect of family: Am I putting myself or my needs before those of my family? What effort am I making for my family's spiritual good when it requires personal sacrifice?

Love of the world and material things: Have I allowed my love of worldly things become an idol in my heart? Am I willing to be generous with my money and possessions?

Pride: Do I have vanity about my appearance? Do I spend more time getting ready for church rather than preparing my heart and mind to worship God when I get there? Am I offended, or even slightly irritated, if others don't notice my appearance?

Envy: Do I struggle with hearing others praised? Am I jealous of those who seem more fruitful or gifted or recognizable than I am?

A critical spirit: Do I use my spirit of discernment to find fault with others who don't measure up to my standards or expectations?

Slander: Do I tell the truth with the intention of causing people to think less of another person? Whose faults, real or imagined, have I discussed behind their backs? Why have I done this?

Lack of seriousness toward God: Do I show disrespect for God by the way I sleep through my prayer time or show up late for church as though He doesn't really matter? Do I give Him the leftovers of my emotions, time, thoughts, or money?

Lying: Do I vocalize anything that is contrary to the truth? Do I design deception? What have I said that was designed to impress someone but it wasn't the whole truth or was an exaggeration of the truth?

Cheating: Do I treat others the way I want to be treated myself? Have I stopped short of treating others the way I would want to be treated?

Hypocrisy: Do I pretend to be something or someone I am not? Am I pretending?

Robbing God: Do I spend/waste time on things that have no eternal value? Do I bring my 'whole tithe' to God as taught in His Word?

Temper: Have I lost patience with a child, co-worker, friend, spouse, or staff member? What cross words have I spoken lately? Have I lost control of my emotions, thoughts, and words so that I abuse someone else verbally? Have I lost my temper?

Hindering others: Am I respectful of other people's time, or do I take it needlessly? Have I hurt someone else's confidence because I hold them to an unreasonably high standard?

Arrogance: Do I have a tendency to accept God's forgiveness while refusing to forgive myself or someone else?

Thank you for taking the time to get quiet and alone with the Lord and allow Him to speak to you and examine your heart. This list is meant to be between you and Him.

Perhaps you would take the time to go through it several times and allow His Spirit to continue to speak to you as you 'seek the Lord'.

The list you just worked through is meant to serve as a prompter for you to reflect and ponder your life with the Lord. It is in no way meant to be for condemnation or accusation. The Bible has made it clear that there is no condemnation for those who are in Christ Jesus.

***How wonderful to know that as we confess our sins,
'He is faithful and just to forgive our sins
and to cleanse us from all unrighteousness."***

(1 John 1:9)

A Modern Story of Bravery
Rosa Parks

By refusing to give up her seat to a white man on an Alabama city bus in 1955, African-American seamstress Rosa Parks (1913-2005), helped spark the civil rights movement in the United States.

Rosa was ordered by the bus driver to yield her seat to a white man, after the white section on the bus was filled. In the 1940's, bus drivers carried guns and had 'police power' to rearrange the seating on the bus any way they chose.

As a result of Rosa's subsequent arrest for violating segregation laws, a bus boycott began. Led by a young Rev. Dr. Martin Luther King Jr., the boycott lasted more than a year, and ended only when the U.S. Supreme Court ruled that bus segregation was unconstitutional. It was a heroic effort, and one that demanded tremendous sacrifices. But as a result, they had changed the law and had begun a movement that would change America forever.

Although widely honored in her later years, Rosa suffered for her act. She was fired from her job as a seamstress in a local department store, and she received death threats for years afterwards.

Rosa's faith in God played a great role in her life. She is quoted as saying, "As a child, I learned from the Bible to trust in God and not be afraid. I felt the Lord would give me the strength to endure whatever I had to face. God did away with all my fear."

Psalm 27 was one of her favorite passages, whose first lines read: "The Lord is my light and my salvation; whom shall I fear? The Lord is the strength of my life; of whom shall I be afraid?"

Over the next half century, Rosa Parks became a nationally recognized symbol of dignity and strength in the struggle to end entrenched racial segregation.

She is known for saying:

"I have learned over the years that when one's mind is made up; this diminishes fear; knowing what must be done does away with fear."

Rosa's personal experiences with injustice and lack of equality led her to be brave and to blaze a trail for millions behind her.

Be Brave
WEEK FIVE

The brave woman who reached out for Jesus

I Surrender All

*All to Jesus I surrender, all to Him I freely give;
I will ever love and trust Him, in His presence daily live.*

*Refrain:
I surrender all, I surrender all.
All to Thee, my blessed Savior, I surrender all.*

*All to Jesus I surrender, humbly at His feet I bow,
Worldly pleasures all forsaken, take me, Jesus, take me now.*

Refrain

*All to Jesus I surrender, make me, Savior, wholly Thine;
May Thy Holy Spirit fill me, may I know Thy pow'r divine.*

Refrain

*All to Jesus I surrender, Lord, I give myself to Thee;
Fill me with Thy love and power, let Thy blessing fall on me.*

Refrain

~Judson W. VanDeVenter; Winfield S. Weeden

Day One:

Read Matthew 9:18-22.

1) Summarize the events of this passage as they involve this woman. What are some things that jump out at you? What surprises you? What challenges you?

2) How do you see Jesus responding in this narrative?

3) "She came from behind and touched the hem of His garment." To better understand the background, meaning and spiritual significance of her action, read Numbers 15:37-41.
    - Who directed the children of Israel to make and wear tassels?

    - What was the purpose of the tassels?

4) The visual reminder of the duty to obey the Law was given because of the serious consequences of disobeying the Law. To see an aspect of the Law that directly impacted the woman, read Leviticus 15:19-20 and verse 25.
   What was her label according to the Law?

5) How do you think this label impacted her?
   - Socially-
   - Emotionally-
   - Spiritually-
   - Physically-

Day Two

Read Mark 5:21-34.

This is the same story of the woman with the blood issue, but Mark gives us more information.

1) What new things do you learn from this passage regarding the woman? List them here with the verse reference.

2) How do you think she had 'heard about Jesus' and knew to 'touch the hem of His garment'?

3) What drove her to Jesus?

4) What 4 aspects of her healing do you discover in verse 29?

5) What was Jesus' response to the woman's touch?

6) How did the disciples respond?

Day Three

Read Mark 5:32-34.

1) What does Jesus do in verse 32?

2) What is the response of the woman to Jesus' questioning?

3) The fact that she knew she had been healed caused her to fall down and worship. Read Psalm 89:7 and tell how we see the psalm fulfilled in this encounter with Jesus.

4) What 3 things does Jesus declare to the woman in verse 34?

5) Along with healing her, Jesus also gives her peace. His healing of her is both outward and inward. Read Luke 1:78-79 and read the last part of Zacharias' prophecy. In what ways do we see this prophecy fulfilled in this encounter?

Day Four

Read Luke 8: 43-48.

1) What new piece of information do you learn from this passage regarding the woman and her situation?

2) The Greek word used for healed in this passage is therapeuo, where we get our words therapy and therapeutic. The word eventually came to mean to heal, restore to health, to cure. What means had the woman used and ultimately exhausted to find her therapeuo?

3) What about you? Do you have a story to tell in regards to your own healing? What is your typical response or reaction when you have a health issue?

4) In verse 44, we learn that the woman came from behind to touch Jesus. Why do you think she did that, based on your study so far?

5) In verse 45 Jesus wants to know who touched Him. Do you think He knew who touched Him, or do you think He needed to ask? Why or why not?

6) List the events that followed after Jesus' question. After you've finished your list, explain why you think Jesus had to ask the question, 'who touched me?'

Day Five

Take the time to re-read the passages from this week's study.

1) Explain why you think the woman with the issue of blood was so brave.

2) Tell what application you can make in your own life as you have spent this week studying this woman's pilgrimage to Jesus.

3) As we come to the end of our study on bravery, take the time today to review the previous weeks of homework. Take a highlighter marker to the lessons you gleaned from each chapter. Be ready to share with your group on this final day of meeting together, your own personal highlights of Be Brave.

4) How are you different after having done this study?

5) Write out a prayer using some of your favorite Scripture from this study, and ask the Lord to cultivate His Spirit of bravery, courage and faith in your heart. Use this prayer in the coming days and weeks as way to 'seal' the lessons you've learned from this study.

A Modern Story of Bravery
Yusra Mardini

Many people are alive today, thanks to the efforts of Yusra Mardini and her sister. The sisters were fleeing Syria along with 18 other people when the refugees' dinghy began sinking in the Aegean Sea as they tried to get to Greece.

The motor had failed, and no one on the boat could swim except for the sisters. It's a story that often ends in tragedy, but these two swimming sisters made sure that would not happen.

The two women leapt out of the boat into the cold waters, and swam as they pushed the boat three hours into the open water in order to prevent it from capsizing. They eventually made it to land.

Yusra said, "I remember that without swimming, I would never be alive, maybe because of the story of this boat. It's a positive memory for me."

Yusra went on to compete in the Summer Olympics of 2016 for the refugee team. She continues to work tirelessly, not only on her swimming, but also in changing the perception of refugees around the world.

Yusra said, "I want everyone to think refugees are normal people who had their homelands and lost them, not because they wanted to run away and be refugees, but because they have dreams in their lives and they had to go."

Fleeing a life-and-death situation, along with pursuing her dreams, has enabled Yusra to be brave.

Works Cited

The Amplified Bible, La Habra, CA: The Lockman Foundation, 2015. Print.

Kelly-Gange, Carol. "Quotable Wisdom; Mother Teresa." Fall River Press Publishers. 2014.

Lotz, Anne Graham. "The Daniel Prayer; Prayer that moves heaven and changes nations." Zondervan Publishers. 2016.

The Hymnal for Worship and Celebration, Waco, TX. Word Music. 1986

The New Spirit-Filled Life Bible. Nashville, TN. Thomas Nelson Publishers, 2002. Print.

History.com website. Retrieved September 17, 2016.

Sbnation.com. Retrieved September 17, 2016.

About the Author

Marjie Schaefer believes the Word of God is relevant, powerful, transformational, and life-giving to every single human being on the planet. She has spent her life investing in others and inviting them to join her in this pursuit of deeper truth.

As a result of her passion and pursuit, she has spent decades teaching women of all ages how to dig into the Word of God, and how to mine the treasures of it for themselves. She started in college and has continued on as a wife and mom, opening her heart and her home to those who hunger and thirst for more of God and His Word in their lives.

Marjie and her team currently lead the ministry, Flourish Through The Word, which is a community of women in the greater Seattle region committed to being equipped through God's Word. As a result of their time together in the Word, the women then move out into their arenas of influence, shining their lights for Jesus. You can find out more about this ministry and upcoming events and Bible studies at www.flourishthroughtheword.com .

Marjie has several published studies; <u>Grace Encounters</u>, <u>Choose Joy</u>, <u>Live Happy</u>, <u>Just Jesus</u>, and <u>I Believe in the Name of Jesus.</u> These are available on Amazon.

Marjie has been married to Steve for 29 years and together they have four children: a daughter Hayley, a son Jordan, and twin sons, Matthew and Luke.

www.ingramcontent.com/pod-product-compliance
Lightning Source LLC
Chambersburg PA
CBHW082224010526
44113CB00037B/2522